Yes in My Backyard

How States and Local Communities Can Find Common Ground in Expanding Housing Choice and Opportunity

Stockton Williams, Lisa Sturtevant, and Rosemarie Hepner

Urban Land Institute

Terwilliger Center for Housing

About the Urban Land Institute

The Urban Land Institute is a global, member-driven organization comprising more than 40,000 real estate and urban development professionals dedicated to advancing the Institute's mission of providing leadership in the responsible use of land and creating and sustaining thriving communities worldwide.

ULI's interdisciplinary membership represents all aspects of the industry, including developers, property owners, investors, architects, urban planners, public officials, real estate brokers, appraisers, attorneys, engineers, financiers, and academics. Established in 1936, the Institute has a presence in the Americas, Europe, and Asia Pacific regions, with members in 80 countries.

The extraordinary impact that ULI makes on land use decision making is based on its members sharing expertise on a variety of factors affecting the built environment, including urbanization, demographic and population changes, new economic drivers, technology advancements, and environmental concerns.

Peer-to-peer learning is achieved through the knowledge shared by members at thousands of convenings each year that reinforce ULI's position as a global authority on land use and real estate. In 2016 alone, more than 1,700 events were held in 250 cities around the world.

Drawing on the work of its members, the Institute recognizes and shares best practices in urban design and development for the benefit of communities around the globe.

More information is available at uli.org. Follow ULI on Twitter, Facebook, LinkedIn, and Instagram.

Cover photos (clockwise from top left): ©Feverpitched www.AndyDeanPhotography.com; ©FangXiaNuo; ©monkeybusinessimages; ©castillodominici.

Recommended bibliographic listing:
Williams, Stockton, Lisa Sturtevant, and Rosemarie Hepner. *Yes in My Backyard: How States and Local Communities Can Find Common Ground in Expanding Housing Choice and Opportunity*. Washington, DC: Urban Land Institute, 2017.

ISBN: 978-0-87420-407-0

Urban Land Institute
2001 L Street, NW, Suite 200
Washington, DC 20036-4948

About the ULI Terwilliger Center for Housing

The ULI Terwilliger Center for Housing conducts research, performs analysis, and develops best practice and policy recommendations that reflect the land use and development priorities of ULI members across all residential product types. The center's mission is to facilitate creating and sustaining a full spectrum of housing opportunities—including workforce and affordable housing—in communities across the United States. The center was founded in 2007 with a gift from longtime ULI member and former ULI chairman J. Ronald Terwilliger.

Acknowledgments

The following ULI members, staff, and other experts provided valuable assistance with this report: Douglas Abbey (Swift Real Estate Partners), Cathy Bennet (ULI Minnesota), Caren Dewar (ULI Minnesota), Hal Ferris (Spectrum Development Solutions), David Fink (Partnership for Strong Communities), Sean Ghio (Partnership for Strong Communities), Mike Kent (Office of Housing for the city of Seattle), Margaux LeClair (Massachusetts Department of Housing and Community Development), Adam Long (Smith Hartvigsen PLLC), Linda Mandolini (Eden Housing), Edward H. Marchant (EHM/Real Estate Adviser), Dara Kovel (Beacon Communities Development), William Reyelt (Massachusetts Department of Housing and Community Development), Laura Shufelt (Massachusetts Housing Partnership), and Ben Stillwell (the Grossman Companies).

The views expressed in the study are the Urban Land Institute's alone, as are any errors or omissions. Funding for this study was provided by generous support from the Abbey Research and Educational Endowment, established through a gift to the ULI Foundation.

ULI Senior Executives

Patrick L. Phillips
Global Chief Executive Officer

Michael Terseck
Chief Financial Officer/Chief Administrative Officer

Cheryl Cummins
Global Governance Officer

Ralph Boyd
Chief Executive Officer
ULI Americas

Lisette van Doorn
Chief Executive Officer
ULI Europe

John Fitzgerald
Chief Executive Officer
ULI Asia Pacific

Kathleen B. Carey
President and Chief Executive Officer
ULI Foundation

Adam Smolyar
Chief Marketing and Membership Officer

Stockton Williams
Executive Vice President
Content

Steve Ridd
Executive Vice President
Global Business Operations

Authors

Stockton Williams

Lisa Sturtevant

Rosemarie Hepner

ULI Project Staff

James Mulligan
Senior Editor

David James Rose
Manuscript Editor

Betsy Van Buskirk
Creative Director

Deanna Pineda
Muse Advertising Design
Graphic Designer

Craig Chapman
Senior Director, Publishing Operations

ULI Terwilliger Center for Housing National Advisory Board Members

Foreword

"We shape our buildings and afterwards our buildings shape us."
—Winston Churchill[1]

To paraphrase Churchill, the built environment reflects society's values. We can surely agree on the following important values, which support the American Dream:

Melting Pot (e *pluribus unum*):

1. Economic mobility (ability to advance up the income ladder irrespective of background);

2. Housing choice (housing type and tenure to meet a variety of human needs); and

3. Housing affordability (housing costs that do not consume an excessive share of income).

Do our land use patterns support these values and aspirations? To answer this question, it is helpful to review the history of land use regulation.

Zoning ordinances first appeared in 1916 in New York City in reaction to tall buildings that blocked access to light and air. Zones restricting land use by type were established to separate industrial uses from places of residence. Such ordinances were hotly contested as an infringement on property rights. The controversy bubbled up in the landmark case *Euclid v. Ambler*. A lower court presciently stated:

> The purpose to be accomplished is really to regulate the mode of living . . . and to classify the population and segregate them according to their income or situation in life.[2]

However, the U.S. Supreme Court in 1926 ruled that land use regulation was a legitimate use of the "police power" to protect the health and safety of residents.

In the 1920s, the federal government promulgated model state legislation to regulate land use. The standard framework was zoning ordinances to control and restrict land use. For the last 80 years, land use decisions have been delegated from the state to local jurisdictions. What has been the result?

Let's turn to simple economics. Assume you are a homeowner in a desirable neighborhood. If supply is restricted, the value of your home goes up. The majority of voters in suburban jurisdictions are homeowners. It should come as no surprise that local zoning provisions favor large-lot single-family homes and discourage denser attached and rental housing.

Restrictions on supply result in housing cost increases and limited choices for prospective residents across the income spectrum. A critical antidote to high housing cost is greater density and smaller units. Yet the housing that is built is geared to the higher price points of the existing community.

What does it look like on the ground? Communities are becoming increasingly segregated by race and income. Housing choice is limited. Where do the teachers, police officers, firefighters, and baristas who serve our communities live?

And in many jurisdictions around the country, we are building fewer units than demanded, placing pressure on the existing housing stock and raising housing costs for everyone. California provides a case in point. Through the general plan process, regional housing needs are allocated to individual jurisdictions to accommodate growth. Yet local jurisdictions have supplied only 47 percent of the projected housing needs.[3] An extreme case is the San Francisco Bay area, where only 94,000 housing units were permitted despite there being over 530,000 jobs created since 2011.[4]

And what about the less fortunate? We are increasingly seeing children in the lowest quintile confined to neighborhoods that compound disadvantages. Children brought up in low-income urban neighborhoods may be subject to trauma that has severe lifelong impacts on health as well as on economic and educational achievement. Yet when lower-income children are relocated to suburban locations with good schools, there is a significant increase in health and educational attainment.

It is clear that the values of housing affordability, diversity, economic mobility, and opportunity are under siege. Land use plays an important part.

What is the solution? In simple terms, the "state giveth and the state can taketh." States can shift the pendulum away from complete control of land use at the local level. States can exert their authority to promote the economic health and well-being of the population by providing incentives and disincentives to local jurisdictions to meet their fair share of housing needs. Policy responses fall into three categories:

1. Encouraging delivery of a range of housing choices;

2. Avoiding state measures that add to the cost of housing; and

3. Promoting new construction of affordable housing through a variety of federal, state, and local subsidies.

While direct subsidy is an effective way of delivering affordability, it is akin to a lottery where a limited number of residents receive a benefit and the broader population suffers from high housing costs. Resources to deliver subsidized housing are quite limited. By far the most effective means of addressing housing choice and affordability is to incentivize jurisdictions to meet their fair share of housing need.

The following report analyzes techniques that can be used at the state level to improve housing choice and affordability.

Douglas Abbey
Lecturer in Real Estate, Stanford Graduate School of Business
Trustee of the Urban Land Institute

Contents

Introduction

Rising housing costs are creating hardships for millions of households and taking a toll on economic growth and productivity. One major reason for the worsening housing affordability problem is that we are simply not building enough housing as a nation, especially in the job-rich regions where housing demand is greatest.

Local zoning and land use regulations, and the related development review processes, make it increasingly difficult to build new housing in many communities, leading to inadequate housing supply and higher housing costs. Edward Glaeser, a Harvard economist and ULI trustee, recently noted:

> Reforming local land use controls is one of those rare areas in which the libertarian and the progressive agree. The current system restricts the freedom of the property owner and also makes life harder for poorer Americans. The politics of zoning reform may be hard, but our land use regulations are badly in need of rethinking.[5]

Some communities are, in fact, trying to reduce the regulatory burden on housing development. Austin, Minneapolis, and San Diego are among cities that recently have reduced fees, streamlined approvals, and provided incentives to encourage construction and rehabilitation. ULI district councils are encouraging local officials in a number of other cities to follow their lead.

Most communities seem unlikely to act with the necessary efficacy on their own, though. The federal government, which plays a limited role in local land use, is not likely to be much help. State government, however, can be a much more constructive partner with local jurisdictions than is generally understood. This largely overlooked opportunity is the focus of this report.

We identify five specific ways that states can help localities foster a healthier housing market, through land use and related policies, with examples of at least partial success by states in implementing each. Some of these state-led initiatives are longstanding; others are newer. These approaches could almost certainly be adopted by any number of other states to spur creation of more housing. A state that put all five approaches together would likely see significant improvements in communities facing a housing shortfall.

At a time when states and cities are often at odds over hotly contested social and economic issues, land use reform to expand housing choice and opportunity can constitute common ground. State and local collaboration on housing can create a lower cost of doing business, a more efficient real estate market, and a wider array of options for buyers and renters across the income spectrum.

Section I: Where We Are and How We Got Here

This section provides a summary of the current housing supply shortage, the evolution and impact of local zoning on housing development, and the context for state involvement in local land use policy making.

The Housing Supply Shortage

In the United States, more than one in four renters, or 11.1 million households, are severely cost burdened, paying half or more of their income for housing.[6] The Joint Center for Housing Studies at Harvard University has estimated that over the next ten years, more than 1.3 million additional households will be severely cost burdened.[7]

Housing affordability challenges are not limited to a few high-cost cities on the coasts, although the competition for housing in the nation's fast-growing coastal regions has accelerated at an alarming rate since the Great Recession. For example, in 2015, nearly 30 percent of renters in California and New York were severely cost burdened. But rates of severe cost burden among renters exceeded 25 percent in a diverse set of states, ranging from Alabama and Louisiana to Oregon and New Mexico.[8]

The primary driver of the growing housing affordability challenge is an insufficient supply of housing to meet demand in places where people want to live and have jobs. In 2016, new residential starts nationwide totaled 1.17 million, up 5.6 percent over 2015 but still far below the 20-year annual average of 1.32 million starts.[9]

Figure 1. Permits for New Housing Units Are Below Historic Averages in Many States

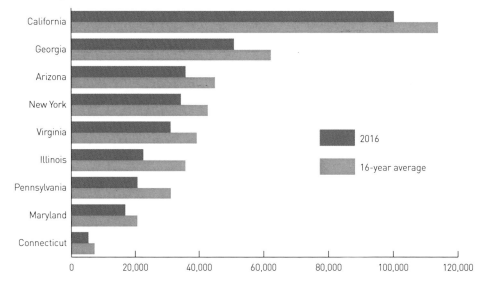

Source: U.S. Census Bureau and U.S. Department of Housing and Urban Development; Building Permits Survey, Permits by State, Annual Data; downloaded from https://www.census.gov/construction/bps/stateannual.html (26 July 2017).

The National Association of Realtors estimates that the country's supply of for-sale and rental units combined is 3 million units short of current demand (figure 1).[10]

In California, where extensive analysis of the housing shortfall has been done, the Legislative Analyst's Office (LAO) has concluded that the state needs to nearly double the rate of planned housing production and build about 100,000 more units *each year* than currently projected, primarily in coastal metropolitan areas, in order to meet the demand from job and population growth.[11] In dozens of other states—from Connecticut to Maryland to Illinois to Arizona—the level of new residential construction remains far below long-term averages and what is needed to keep up with demand.[12]

Several factors are driving the housing shortfall, ranging from construction labor shortages in the wake of the Great Recession to declining public subsidies for low-cost housing dating back even further. Over the past decade or so, economists across the ideological spectrum have agreed about another cause: the increased cost of local zoning and other regulations. As Joseph Gyourko and Raven Molloy observed in 2014: "Regulation appears to raise house prices, reduce construction, reduce the elasticity of housing supply, and alter urban form."[13] Gyourko and Molloy found little evidence that benefits of land use regulations can offset the negative impacts, including reduced housing supply and affordability.

The Evolution and Impact of Local Zoning

Land use is heavily determined by zoning regulations, which have historically been established and administered at the local level. Zoning effectively dictates the quantity and types of development that can be built in a community.

The localization of zoning originated in communities' need to manage growth from industrialization in the late 19th and early 20th centuries,

though the goal of exclusion was also part of early ordinances. For example, San Francisco established "no-laundry" zones in 1886; ostensibly intended to ensure fire safety, they also served to segregate Chinese immigrants.[14] New York City's tenement laws led to the establishment of building codes in 1916 intended to protect against overcrowding and poor building quality.[15] By the mid-1920s, almost 400 local municipalities had adopted zoning ordinances.[16]

Modern zoning by land use category evolved from these earlier ordinances as a way to protect residents from the noise, smog, and other perceived nuisances emitted from various urban industries. It separated land uses into types (e.g., residential, commercial, industrial) and put limits on the amount and form of development that could occur in different places in the city.

Euclidean zoning, as it is known, emerged from the landmark Supreme Court case *Euclid v. Ambler* (1926). When the village of Euclid, Ohio, established the town's first zoning ordinance in 1922, it zoned the area encompassing land owned by Ambler Realty Company for nonindustrial uses. Ambler had bought the land specifically to sell for industrial purposes and argued that the zoning would reduce the land's value and cause him financial hardship. The court upheld the village of Euclid's zoning.

After *Euclid v. Ambler*, local zoning continued to take on even greater importance in shaping the physical growth and development of communities. Zoning ordinances included requirements related to setbacks, lot lines, building bulk, and parking. Zoning rules restricted development to account for floodplains and other environmental concerns, as well as for purposes of historic preservation.

While zoning can be motivated by legitimate public interests, it can also excessively restrict housing development and significantly drive up housing costs. Jason Furman, former chairman of the White House Council of Economic Advisors, summarized the point succinctly in 2015:

Zoning restrictions—be they in the form of minimum lot sizes, off-street parking requirements, height limits, prohibitions on multifamily housing, or lengthy permitting processes—are supply constraints. Basic economic theory predicts—and many empirical studies confirm—that housing markets in which supply cannot keep up with demand will see housing prices rise.... [I]n addition to constraining supply, zoning shifts demand outward, exerting further upward pressure on prices and thus economic rents, too.[17]

The local development process has increasingly involved public input, which has amplified the impact of local rules about land use and zoning. A large body of research has shown that existing residents often use zoning and other land use controls to limit or prevent new development in their neighborhoods.[18] Driven by self-interest, residents—typically homeowners but increasingly existing renters—work to limit new development that they think will reduce their property values, change the character of their neighborhood, or otherwise negatively affect their quality of life.

The State Role in Local Land Use

Throughout zoning's history, there has been little direction or interference from the federal or state government in setting land use regulations. States, however, have more power in this area than may be commonly understood.[19] The U.S. Constitution stipulates that any powers not specifically reserved for the federal government are granted to states, such as land use laws. Local governments must be granted powers by the state; otherwise, they remain in the state's authority.

Different states have established different statutory relationships with their municipalities. States that permit municipalities broad local

Home Rule vs. Dillon's Rule

<u>Home Rule States:</u>

Alaska, Florida,* Iowa, Massachusetts, Montana, New Jersey, New Mexico, Ohio, Oregon, South Carolina, and Utah

<u>Dillon's Rule States:</u>

Arizona, Arkansas, Connecticut, Delaware, Georgia, Hawaii, Idaho, Kentucky, Maine, Maryland, Michigan, Minnesota, Mississippi, Missouri, Nebraska, Nevada, New Hampshire, New York, North Carolina, North Dakota, Oklahoma, Pennsylvania, Rhode Island, South Dakota, Texas, Vermont, Virginia, West Virginia, Washington, Wisconsin, and Wyoming (all municipalities)

Alabama, California, Colorado, Illinois, Indiana, Louisiana, and Tennessee (only for certain municipalities)

*Florida employs home rule, but the state maintains taxing authority.

Source: National League of Cities, "Cities 101—Delegation of Power," accessed from http://www.nlc.org/resource/cities-101-delegation-of-power (2 August 2017).

autonomy are known as "Home Rule" states. "Dillon's Rule" states maintain a stricter interpretation, severely limiting autonomy of local governments to only those authorities that the state has either expressly granted or "fairly implied." In either statutory framework, states have the ability to extend their authority into local decisions if broad public benefits are associated with that involvement. Yet, states have rarely taken proactive roles in the local regulation of land use through legislative or regulatory actions.

The most significant legal cases involving state intervention in local zoning were the "Mount Laurel" decisions by the New Jersey Supreme

Court in 1975 and 1983. Those decisions declared that local land use regulations that prevent affordable housing opportunities for low-income people are unconstitutional. The court required all New Jersey municipalities to plan, zone for, and take affirmative actions to provide realistic opportunities for their "fair share" of the region's need for affordable housing for low- and moderate-income people.

In 1985, the New Jersey State Legislature enacted the Fair Housing Act, which created the Council on Affordable Housing (COAH) to establish "fair share" housing requirements for localities. Between 1986 and 1999, the COAH process engendered intense litigation among municipalities, builders, and affordable housing advocates. In 1999, COAH effectively stopped functioning as a result of political and legal battles. In January 2017, more than 40 years after the original Mount Laurel decision, the New Jersey Supreme Court ruled that New Jersey towns must collectively provide tens of thousands of new affordable housing units over the next decade, making up for their failure to do so since 1999.

While the court's January 2017 ruling ostensibly removes the primary obstacles to the implementation of the state's fair share housing requirements, it remains largely unclear at present how towns will meet a nearly two-decade backlog of unmet housing development.

The Mount Laurel case suggests that state courts can force local action in the absence of state policy. At the same time, the case demonstrates how challenging it can be for states to impose mandatory housing requirements on localities. Not surprisingly, according to one recent analysis only a few states "have stepped in and adopted mandatory policies that require zoning reform for affordable housing production . . . aimed at curbing exclusionary zoning, ensuring a fair share of affordable units in communities, and increasing the regionwide supply of affordable housing."[20] However, a range of options are available to states and local communities to work together to expand housing opportunity. These are the focus of the next section.

Section II: Five Ways States Can Support Healthier Local Housing Markets

Every state has the authority and resources to help localities plan for and accommodate the housing they need through land use and zoning policies. However, relatively few states and local communities seem to be aware of what is possible or have been reluctant to seize opportunities for collaboration.

This report aims to change that dynamic through brief case studies of several state-led initiatives and an assessment of what they suggest for implementation elsewhere. While the political, legal, economic, and development environments are different from state to state, there is good reason to believe that the broad approaches profiled here could be adapted widely.

The report reviews five types of opportunities for states to help cities and counties expand housing choice and opportunity principally through their land use powers. These opportunities include both "carrots" and "sticks"—that is, incentives and consequences—to promote the development of sufficient housing.

Figure 2. Complementary State Strategies for Smarter Local Land Use

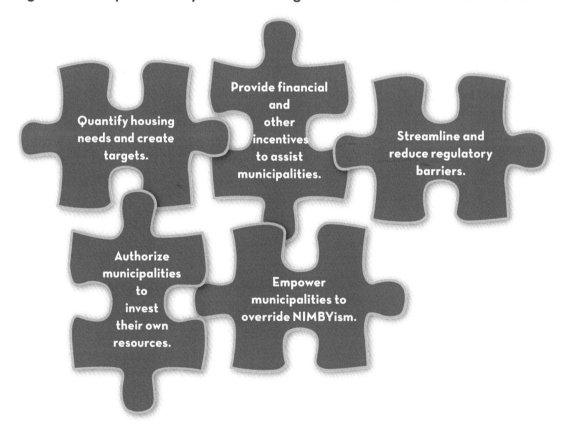

Quantify housing needs and create targets.

Provide financial and other incentives to assist municipalities.

Streamline and reduce regulatory barriers.

Authorize municipalities to invest their own resources.

Empower municipalities to override NIMBYism.

Source: Urban Land Institute.

Based on this review, more states can and should:

1. **Ensure that localities and regions are assessing their housing needs for the future.** Because many communities do not analyze their housing needs or assess the importance of housing to economic growth, states should establish and enforce workable standards.

2. **Provide incentives to local communities to zone for new housing.** Zoning often needs to be modified to allow for and encourage development of needed new housing. States can support communities' efforts with financial and technical assistance.

3. **Reduce regulatory requirements that increase costs and stifle development.** States can use their authority and creativity to cut the regulatory red tape that unnecessarily makes housing more expensive.

4. **Authorize municipalities to invest their own resources linked to pro-housing land use.** Even with appropriate zoning, local jurisdictions often need state approval to offer their own incentives for construction of below-market-rate housing.

5. **Enable local communities to overcome unreasonable neighborhood opposition.** Community opposition can drive up the cost of—or completely derail—the construction of new housing. States can provide mechanisms to moderate "not in my backyard" (NIMBY) opposition and make it easier to build housing needed to support local growth.

These strategies all relate to creating a more favorable environment for housing development mainly through local land use policy. States also provide an array of funding and financing for housing development and rehabilitation more broadly. While those policies and programs— such as tax credits, tax-exempt bonds, and state block grants—are beyond the scope of this report, they can be and are often used in the context of the land use strategies profiled here.

1 Ensure That Localities and Regions Are Assessing Their Housing Needs for the Future

States should ensure that localities are regularly assessing their housing needs and zoning appropriately to accommodate expected growth. California's experience suggests that such a policy can spur useful local planning and analysis—but, on its own, it is insufficient for driving the amount of necessary new development.

California's Regional Housing Needs Allocation Process

Quantifying the housing needed in a local community is a critical first step to ensuring that a sufficient amount of housing gets built. Since 1969, every city and county in California has been required to develop a general plan, which includes a plan "element" specifically for land use and housing that identifies and quantifies current and future housing needs.[21] Plans are developed either every five or every eight years, and are developed through a collaborative state/local process. The state's Department of Housing and Community Development (HCD) begins the process by determining housing needs by income levels for every region across the state. HCD calculates future household growth by income group for each regional council of governments (COG).

Through a process called the regional housing needs allocation (RHNA), every jurisdiction is allocated its "fair share" of housing. Localities must then update their housing plans to reflect their housing target and lay out strategies for meeting the projected demand. As part of the process, the COGs and local jurisdictions engage with stakeholders, and the housing needs allocation is developed with considerable public comment.

RHNA technically is linked to other California laws that are intended to drive local action based

Figure 3. California Communities Have Fallen Far Short of Meeting Affordable Housing Demand

RHNA Performance by Select Jurisdictions, 2003–2014

Jurisdiction	Target total	Total completed	% Achieved
San Diego COG	107,300	90,545	84.4%
Los Angeles	280,907	115,775	41.2%
Orange	82,332	45,846	55.7%
Riverside	174,705	92,635	53.0%
San Bernardino	107,543	44,843	41.7%
San Francisco	31,193	19,868	63.7%
Contra Costa	27,072	15,478	57.2%
Santa Clara	60,338	33,399	55.4%
Sacramento	59,094	26,965	45.6%
Fresno COG	52,142	24,970	47.9%
Kern COG	41,640	26,578	63.8%
Total	**1,024,266**	**536,902**	**52.4%**

Source: California Department of Housing and Community Development, "California's Housing Future: Challenges and Opportunities, Public Draft - Statewide Housing Assessment 2025," 2017.

Note: Jurisdictions listed above are counties unless specified as council of government (COG) regions.

on the needs allocation. For example, under the state's density bonus law, local governments must rezone, if necessary, to provide sufficient capacity in higher-density zones to accommodate their RHNA targets for lower-income households. In addition, local jurisdictions cannot deny a project affordable to moderate-, low-, and very low-income households if the jurisdiction's housing element is not in compliance with state law.

Although the RHNA process emphasizes comprehensive local housing planning, the planning process by itself has not led to the development of sufficient housing to meet needs in California. From 2003 through 2014, no region in California met its RHNA target and the state overall built only 47 percent of the housing required to meet projected need, according to the California HCD.[22] In addition, the state's LAO found that roughly 20 percent of communities in the state either adopted a noncompliant housing plan or simply did not submit a plan at all.[23] While the state can withhold housing-related state funds or suspend local permitting authority until completed plans are submitted, enforcement of these sanctions has been minimal.

Virginia's Statewide Regional Housing Assessment

While California's RHNA process is longstanding, other states are just beginning the process of requiring or encouraging local housing needs assessments. In Virginia, the Department of Housing and Community Development, Department of Commerce, along with the state housing finance agency, the Virginia Housing Development Authority, are coordinating with state universities and partners at the local level to conduct a statewide assessment of current and future housing needs.

As part of the assessment, Virginia has funded a study of the quantity of new housing that would be needed in 11 regions to support anticipated job growth. In addition, the state is funding and coordinating a housing gap analysis conducted by Virginia Tech for each metropolitan area in the state. The gap analysis will assess the extent of housing cost burden and overcrowding in each region, and will identify the amount of additional housing that would be needed in each metropolitan area to close the housing gap.

The results from the state-sponsored regional housing needs assessments are designed to be used by local jurisdictions for planning purposes. In addition, the project's emphasis on the link between housing and economic development is intended to help provide a new approach for building local support for new housing construction. The results from the regional housing needs assessments and gap analyses will be presented at the 2017 Virginia Governor's Housing Conference in November.

Takeaways

Assessing housing needs alone does not lead to sufficient construction; however, this type of local analysis remains valuable to help communities better understand their housing markets. A 2016 report from the Terner Center for Housing Innovation at the University of California, Berkeley, noted that "the RHNA process accounts for variations in housing needs across California's diverse housing markets and provides for an established data and reporting system."[24]

And some evidence exists that there can be an impact on the amounts or locations of new housing as a result of housing needs assessments. An analysis by the University of California, Davis, found that "the authority tasked with distributing RHNA for the Bay Area successfully distributed new affordable housing units in jurisdictions with greater jobs-housing imbalances when compared to the distribution of market-rate production in the same period."[25]

While a state-required and state-supported local housing needs analysis and housing production target may generate useful analysis, and

is critical in places where these assessments are not routinely done, the California experience makes clear that analysis and goals alone will not lead to all the necessary housing development. Development incentives, combined with enforceable requirements, are ultimately needed.

2 Provide Incentives to Local Communities to Zone for New Housing

Many communities lack the expertise and wherewithal to exercise their zoning authority in ways that would stimulate needed development. States should provide a zoning framework, technical assistance, and modest financial incentives to help communities develop appropriate zoning standards to produce the housing that is needed. Connecticut and Massachusetts have shown that such efforts can have constructive impacts.

Connecticut Incentive Housing Zones

Adopted in 2006, the Connecticut Incentive Housing Zones (IHZs) program provides municipalities with technical assistance and financial incentives to create zoning districts that can accommodate additional housing. The program's objective is to help cities and towns plan for and create mixed-income residential zones with homes affordable to moderate-income households, specifically designed to attract and retain young professionals, working families, retirees, and residents in critical local professions (e.g., firefighters and teachers) who would otherwise be unable to find housing they can afford in the municipalities they serve.

Twenty percent of units in new residential projects within the local incentive housing zone must be set aside for households earning 80 percent of area median income (AMI) or less, and homes

Figure 4. Interest among Connecticut Towns in Incentive Housing Zones Is Growing

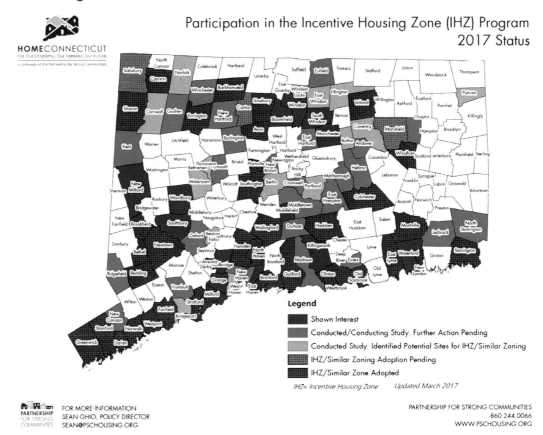

Participation in the Incentive Housing Zone (IHZ) Program
2017 Status

Legend

- Shown Interest
- Conducted/Conducting Study: Further Action Pending
- Conducted Study: Identified Potential Sites for IHZ/Similar Zoning
- IHZ/Similar Zoning Adoption Pending
- IHZ/Similar Zone Adopted

IHZ= Incentive Housing Zone   *Updated March 2017*

FOR MORE INFORMATION
SEAN GHIO, POLICY DIRECTOR
SEAN@PSCHOUSING.ORG

PARTNERSHIP FOR STRONG COMMUNITIES
860.244.0066
WWW.PSCHOUSING.ORG

Source: Partnership for Strong Communities.

must remain affordable for 30 years.

The program is voluntary for municipalities; however, localities can receive up to $20,000 from the state for activities involved in planning for IHZs (e.g., feasibility studies for necessary infrastructure, planning and design standards, legal expenses) and up to $50,000 for mixed-income housing activities (e.g., costs for land purchase options, preliminary engineering costs, appraisals, costs of permits and approvals). In addition, upon adoption of the IHZ, a grant of $50,000 is awarded to the municipalities from the state, with additional funds for each multifamily or single-family unit built.

As of July 2016, more than 40 percent of the state's municipalities have received planning grants to identify appropriate locations for IHZs, draft zoning regulations, and prepare design standards.[26] In the Connecticut towns that have adopted IHZs and similar approaches, 1,700 housing units have been developed.[28]

Massachusetts Smart Growth Zoning Overlay (Chapter 40R)

The forerunner of the Connecticut IHZ program was Massachusetts General Law Chapter 40R, or the "Massachusetts Smart Growth Zoning Overlay District Act," enacted in 2004. While a handful of states had previously passed laws requiring communities to use their zoning powers to support affordable housing development

Downtown Windsor Locks, Connecticut

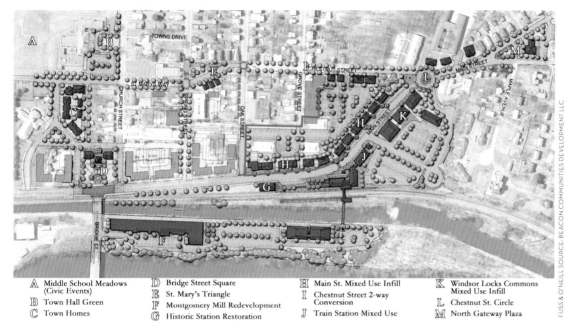

A Middle School Meadows (Civic Events)
B Town Hall Green
C Town Homes
D Bridge Street Square
E St. Mary's Triangle
F Montgomery Mill Redevelopment
G Historic Station Restoration
H Main St. Mixed Use Infill
I Chestnut Street 2-way Conversion
J Train Station Mixed Use
K Windsor Locks Commons Mixed Use Infill
L Chestnut St. Circle
M North Gateway Plaza

The town of Windsor Locks, Connecticut, used its zoning authority and incentives from the Connecticut Incentive Housing Zone program to catalyze a transit-oriented redevelopment of the downtown, including the conversion of the Montgomery Mill property into 160 mixed-income apartments by Beacon Communities. "The town had already taken many steps to make housing development downtown easy," says Dara Kovel, president of Beacon Communities Development LLC. "The zoning framework made our approval process straightforward and speedy. The proactive approach in conjunction with state policy was a green light for our proposal."

(including Massachusetts itself), 40R was the first effort in the country by a state to provide a monetary incentive-based policy to encourage localities to rezone for sufficient housing.

Chapter 40R encourages local communities to establish special zoning overlay districts that allow minimum densities of eight units per acre for single-family homes, 12 units per acre for townhouses, and 20 units per acre for condominiums and apartments. To receive assistance from the state, the zoning must require that 20 percent of the homes in the district be affordable to households earning less than 80 percent of AMI, and mixed-use development is encouraged.[29]

The state provides assistance to towns in crafting and designing their policies. In addition, when municipalities adopt appropriate zoning and put in place a streamlined development process for 40R districts, they are eligible for

$10,000 to $600,000 in state funding, plus an additional $3,000 for every new home built in the new district. A companion state law (Massachusetts General Law 40S) authorizes the state to provide limited reimbursements to local communities for costs of educating new students living in housing built under 40R.

Since its adoption, more than 3,300 units have been built or are in construction across 24 of the 35 communities that have one or more approved 40R districts, and the state's Department of Housing and Community Development estimates that the planned projects are expected to yield another 1,000 to 1,500 units in the near term.[30]

Takeaways

The Massachusetts and Connecticut programs are appealing ways to encourage localities to rezone for additional development of affordable and workforce housing because they are voluntary and incentive based. While the actual amount of new development spurred by IHZ and 40R is small, the former program is relatively new and the latter was launched just before the Great Recession. The increase in communities expressing interest suggests that the policy approach has merit and more upside potential.

In Connecticut, some towns that have not yet adopted an IHZ have developed similar approaches, such as rules for moderate-income dwelling units in business zones (Greenwich), an open-space affordable housing development/multifamily district (Milford), and workforce housing overlay zones (Simsbury).

Nevertheless, it seems clear that the Connecticut IHZ and Massachusetts 40R incentives on their own are too modest to drive major changes to zoning and development. Incentives need to be more robust, and perhaps combined with enforceable requirements, to have a more meaningful market impact.

3 Reduce Regulatory Requirements That increase Costs and Stifle Development

While cost-driving factors like land and materials are hard for policy makers to influence, states can promote initiatives that lead to lower regulatory and constructions costs in order to facilitate the development of new housing. Minnesota has been a leader in this area. California has recently acted to reduce some unnecessary barriers that will potentially create a substantial number of new units.

The Minnesota Challenge
The "Minnesota Challenge to Lower the Cost of Affordable Housing," a partnership of ULI Minnesota, the Regional Council of Mayors, Minnesota Housing (the state housing finance agency), Enterprise Community Partners, and

State Action Can Also Undermine Local Zoning Initiatives

In 2016, Nashville approved a zoning ordinance, supported by the local chamber of commerce and association of Realtors, requiring new apartment projects that request greater density than allowed under existing zoning to provide some units at below-market rents. The city also dedicated grant funds that developers could access for projects covered by the policy. This local ordinance was challenged at the state level, and the Tennessee House of Representatives passed a bill in spring 2017 that would outlaw the program. The state senate did not act on the measure, but the city faces a legal challenge to implementing the policy.

the McKnight Foundation, began in 2014 as an idea competition. The goal of the Minnesota Challenge was to support innovative problem solving from interdisciplinary teams of housing professionals, resulting in a systematic concept for lowering the cost of developing affordable and workforce housing in Minnesota.

The winning proposal, from the University of Minnesota's Center for Urban and Regional Affairs (CURA), was a project that assessed the development cost drivers associated with state and local regulation, and provided recommendations and technical assistance to reduce or eliminate them.

The regulatory and administrative recommendations included early identification of available development sites; fee reductions and waivers; and streamlined administrative processes. Development recommendations included greater density when appropriate for cost savings; reduced parking requirements; and simplifying specifications for materials.

For Minnesota Housing, reducing the regulatory costs of housing development is a continuing strategic priority. As the agency stated in a 2015 report:

> While the MN Cost Challenge started out as an idea competition, it has turned into an ongoing effort to continually identify and eliminate inefficiencies and unnecessary requirements in the development process. As a leading partner in this initiative, we must start with our own requirements and processes.[31]

Building off the momentum of the Minnesota Challenge, Minnesota Housing noted that while many of the CURA recommendations were not new, their value was "identifying and implementing best practices to address them, which included providing technical assistance to communities to pursue the practices and encouraging regional organizations to incorporate the practices and implementation strategies into their policies and guidelines."[32]

Minnesota Housing has taken other steps to reduce development costs as well. For example, it has adopted "MinnDocs," a uniform set of loan documents and a streamlined approval process that the agency estimates will save roughly $1,000 per unit.

California's Parking Reduction Law

Enacted in 2015, California law AB 744, "the Planning and Zoning Law," directs localities to reduce parking requirements for affordable housing developments located near transit. Parking requirements add to the cost of developing housing and can have a substantial impact on the financial feasibility of developing housing affordable to lower-income households. Reducing the amount of parking that is required as part of new residential developments, particularly new housing targeting lower-income households, can be an important component of reducing development costs, making it easier for developers to provide below-market-rate units.

Alta Mira, Hayward, California

Alta Mira is a 151-unit property developed by Eden Housing as part of a master-planned mixed-income community at the South Hayward BART station in the city of Hayward, California. The city's reduced parking requirements enabled Eden Housing to deliver the project for an estimated $3 million less than would have been the case under typical parking requirements.

The California state law automatically reduces parking requirements for transit-accessible affordable housing projects, without the need for the developer to go through a local approval process for the parking reduction. For 100 percent affordable projects that are within a half-mile of a major transit stop, the law calls for a *maximum* of 0.5 parking space per unit. Similar provisions apply for mixed-income developments and senior-only and special-needs projects with access to transit.

The developer does not need to petition the local jurisdiction for these lower parking requirements; they are automatic as long as the project meets the requirements. Local governments can set higher parking standards only if they conduct a parking study.

As Meea Kang, cofounder of Domus Development and a leading advocate of the policy, put it: "This regulatory change, which costs the state nothing and costs the local jurisdictions nothing, allows for certainty and reduces the cost of affordable housing. It allows us to build more housing units for the same area. We're going to get better cost efficiencies."[33]

California's Accessory Dwelling Units Laws

Another California law makes it less costly to build accessory dwelling units (ADUs), or "granny flats," which can be an important source of affordable housing. These types of backyard residential structures have existed in California (and many other states) for years, but local zoning sharply limited their use, and it has been very expensive for homeowners to build these units. According to the California Department of Housing and Community Development:

> Relaxed regulations and the [relatively low] cost to build an ADU make it a very feasible affordable housing option. A UC Berkeley study noted that one unit of affordable housing in the Bay Area costs about $500,000 to develop whereas an ADU can

range anywhere up to $200,000 on the expensive end in high housing cost areas.[34]

The new laws allow the conversion of garages into dwelling units, permit dwelling units to be erected above garages, and waive separate utility-connection requirements. In addition, the new regulations allow for an ADU to be built up to 1,200 square feet. ADUs within existing structures must be allowed in all single-family residential zones as well. With respect to parking, the new laws state that only one space per ADU or bedroom may be required, and the parking space requirement under certain circumstances may be met by using setback space or as a result of tandem parking.

Local governments seeking to implement the law need to pass an ordinance. As part of the process, they are required to identify sites with appropriate zoning that will accommodate projected housing needs in their regional housing needs allocation.

Takeaways

Finding ways to reduce the cost of development—particularly through reducing regulatory requirements or by making it easier to build lower-cost housing—is a critical component of helping localities promote the development of sufficient housing. Legislation from the state that affects local regulation can provide political cover to local elected officials, making it easier for these regulatory changes to be adopted.

There are several key aspects of zoning requirements that, if responsibly relaxed, could be significant game-changers. Reducing parking requirements is a particularly important strategy, and eliminating the requirement to provide unnecessary parking can reduce development costs by $20,000 to $50,000 per unit in high-cost areas.

Furthermore, many projects do not need as much parking as is currently regulated. An analysis of 68 affordable housing developments in the San Francisco Bay area found that 31 percent of the roughly 9,400 parking spaces were empty at night (when they would most likely be full) and that these spaces had increased aggregate construction costs across the projects by $139 million.[35]

Lower-cost housing options can be important for expanding housing options. While it is hard to estimate the impact of these new laws, the California Legislative Analyst's Office noted the following about ADUs:

> Accessory dwellings provide part of the solution to the housing crisis. They are the only source of housing that can be added within a year at an affordable price, in existing developed communities served by infrastructure … without public subsidy, and action by the State on a few issues will make this possible for tens of thousands of owners to immediately benefit and help their communities.[36]

Looking at the whole spectrum of cost-reducing initiatives should be part of a state effort to help create more opportunities at the local level to build enough housing to meet demand.

4 Authorize Municipalities to Invest Their Own Resources Linked to Pro-Housing Land Use

States can provide local jurisdictions with the flexibility to target resources generated locally to housing development in areas that need it and would benefit as part of a land use planning and zoning process. Washington and Utah are among states that have seen significant local activity through different approaches. A newer approach in Texas appears to hold promise as well.

Washington State's Multifamily Tax Exemption (MFTE)

The ability to exempt or abate property taxes can be an important tool for jurisdictions to promote the development of affordable and workforce housing. Cities often need authorization from the state to implement incentives, such as tax exemption. Under Washington state law, cities may exempt rental or owner-occupied multifamily properties in designated areas from ad valorem property taxes for a period of eight

Figure 5. Washington Multifamily Tax Exemption Has Spurred Development in Seattle

Seattle's Multifamily Property Tax Exemption, 2016 Status

	Total units	Units affordable
Program 1 (1998–2002)	474	215
Program 2 (2004–2008)	1,176	741
Program 3 (2008–2010)	5,925	1,727
Program 4 (2011–October 2015)	17,487	3,943
Program 5 (November 2015–present)	3,518	892
Total	**28,580**	**7,518**

Source: City of Seattle Multifamily Property Tax Exemption Program: 2016 Status Report to City Council, March 30, 2017.

Note: Program 1 is the original program; Program 2 allowed some flexibility of AMI targets depending on number of units set aside; Program 3 marks when the exemption was extended from ten to 12 years; Program 4 continued the 12-year exemption and added further adjustments to AMI levels for different-sized units; Program 5 is program in its current form.

or 12 years. This local property tax exemption is available only in relatively compact, mixed-use neighborhoods with adequate infrastructure and transit options.

Properties benefiting from the 12-year exemption must commit to renting or selling at least 20 percent of units to low- and moderate-income households. Cities have discretion to set the income targeting for properties receiving the eight-year exemption. Rents are not restricted when the tax exemption period expires and may revert to market rate upon lease renewal.

Property tax exemptions can help spur residential development in cities with slower-growing economies and can also promote the development of affordable housing in high-cost markets. For smaller cities like Tacoma, Washington, the MFTE program has been an important tool to generate economic development. For thriving, high-growth markets, especially Seattle, the tax exemption has generated much-needed affordable units (see table on the previous page). As of the end of 2016, Seattle approved MFTE applications for projects that included 7,399 affordable rental units and 119 affordable for-sale units, for a total of 7,518.

Utah Local Redevelopment Agencies

The 1969 "Utah Neighborhood Development Act" authorized communities to use local redevelopment agency funding to revitalize blighted areas.[37] In 1998, state law expanded local funding options to explicitly allow the redevelopment agencies to use tax increment financing (TIF) for redevelopment activities, including affordable housing. In 2000, a 20 percent allocation toward affordable housing was made mandatory for certain types of redevelopment projects. Through this form of municipal finance, cities and counties can invest in specified neighborhoods and development projects by leveraging future tax revenues generated by the redevelopment.

The Utah redevelopment law has always had a significant focus on housing development linked to local land use, even as it has been substantially modified over the years. Since 2000, every blight-based redevelopment project area has been required to allocate at least 20 percent of the funds received by the agency toward affordable housing. Beginning in 2016 for all new redevelopment project areas from which the agency receives more than $100,000 annually, at least 10 percent of TIF proceeds must be used for affordable housing development or rehabilitation.

In addition to the mandatory minimum housing allocation, redevelopment agencies are granted significant power to make expenditures outside project areas for the purpose of replacing housing units lost to development, or increasing, improving, and preserving the affordable housing supply of the community that created the agency.

The redevelopment law has generated significant housing development and rehabilitation in Salt Lake County, the largest county in the state, with roughly one-third of the state's population. A 2014 report found that the 13 redevelopment agencies in the county had supported the development of more than 2,300 units. The redevelopment project areas have the potential to generate over $100 million in funding for housing.[38] In 2016, the Salt Lake City Redevelopment Agency (with the Salt Lake City Council as its governing body) allocated more than $30 million from the agency's budget for affordable and homeless housing needs.

Texas Homestead Preservation District and Reinvestment Zones

In 2005, Texas authorized local communities to use their tax-exempt bond financing, offer density bonuses, or provide other incentives (e.g., tax increment financing) to increase the supply of affordable housing and maintain the affordability of existing housing for low- and moderate-income families in areas with rapidly escalating rents.

The policy was largely unworkable until a set of changes implemented in 2013 that gave local jurisdictions more flexibility.

In December 2015, Austin approved the first Homestead Preservation Districts in the state. As required by the Austin City Council, each district must have fewer than 75,000 residents and a poverty rate at least two times the overall poverty rate for the city. In addition, each census tract in the district must have a median income that is less than 80 percent of the overall median family income in the city.

Austin officials project the first approved district to generate roughly $17 million for affordable housing over the next 20 years.[39] A bill to enable smaller Texas cities to create similar zones was vetoed by Governor Greg Abbott in August.

Takeaways

While federal and state funding is essential, access to a broad range of local funding options is important for communities to help support the development of lower-cost housing. The Washington tax exemption program has been effective in incentivizing development in large and small communities across the state at different stages of economic recovery.

It is conceivable that some of the development would have occurred without the incentive; however, the policy does not appear to have

Reverb, Seattle, Washington

Reverb is an 85-unit, mixed-income property in downtown Seattle. Twenty percent of the units are affordable with the rents between 65 percent and 85 percent of the area's median income, while the rest are market rate. According to the developer, Spectrum Development Solutions, the Multifamily Tax Exemption was instrumental to the financial feasibility of the project.

adverse fiscal effects on the communities that have used it.

In addition to supporting the development of affordable and workforce housing, local tax exemption programs can generate fiscal benefits for jurisdictions. Seattle, which currently has 163 developments receiving tax exemptions, reported: "The combined appraised value of residential improvements for these projects, as determined only during their initial appraisal years during which time new construction value would be calculated, totaled approximately $2.36 billion."[40]

In the case of Utah redevelopment agencies, it appears that tax increment financing has had fairly little impact in spurring housing development outside Salt Lake County. In addition, the state law largely limits the availability of the incentive to distressed neighborhoods in need of revitalization, making it less useful in supporting development in more opportunity-rich areas for families.

There are ways to better leverage the opportunities that local property tax exemptions and other local funding provide to developers. Some affordable housing advocates have suggested that the rent-restricted affordability period should be longer (outlasting the tax exemption). In fact, some cities have combined the MFTE program with land use or zoning changes in exchange for a percentage of the units to remain affordable over the long term.

State Action Can Also Result in Housing Funds Being Diverted to Other Purposes

Florida's William E. Sadowski Affordable Housing Trust Fund has raised revenue for state and local housing programs since 1992. However, only a small share of that revenue has actually been used for housing in recent years. Of the nearly $1.9 billion allocated to the trust funds since 2008-2009, state lawmakers have diverted nearly $1.3 billion (68 percent) to other purposes, including tax breaks and additional spending.[41] Business and real estate groups pushing to restore the money for housing say that a full restoration of the trust fund would generate $3.78 billion in economic activity and could result in the creation of 28,700 jobs.[42]

5 Enable Local Communities to Overcome Unreasonable Neighborhood Opposition

Even in cases where local officials support the production of new housing and the economics make sense for developers, neighborhood opposition can block needed new development, often by putting pressure on local agencies responsible for project approval. Massachusetts

Figure 6. Massachusetts's 40B Program: Total Units Built or Under Construction (1970–2016)

	Total units	Affordable units	Affordable units' share
Rental	50,302	30,264	60%
Ownership	19,147	5,434	28%
Mixed tenure	879	278	32%
Total	**70,328**	**35,976**	**51%**

Source: Edward H. Marchant, EHM/Real Estate Adviser, provided to ULI, September 2017.

has taken on this issue more effectively than any other state.

Massachusetts's Comprehensive Permitting and Zoning Appeal Law

The law (known as Chapter 40B) was adopted in 1969 in response to growing concerns that local zoning was excluding lower-cost housing.[43] The law limits a local municipality's authority during development review processes if the community does not have 10 percent of its total housing units affordable to households earning low and moderate incomes. By allowing projects to bypass established local review processes, the state helps moderate the impact of NIMBYism and enable the production of affordable and workforce housing that would not otherwise have been built.

Under 40B, the state eliminates various barriers in the local zoning processes, streamlining approvals for developers who include affordable units in their projects. Development proposals that provide 20 percent of units affordable to households earning no more than 50 percent of AMI (or 25 percent to households earning no more than 80 percent of AMI) are eligible for this simplified development approval process. The simplified review process was designed to shorten the timeline and reduce the cost of development.

Chapter 40B established a relatively clear process for when the state authority would override local approval processes. First, the developer must show proof that it has received eligibility from a state or federal government subsidy program for the development's affordability component. The plans for the development are then submitted to the local zoning board of appeals (ZBA), which acts as the comprehensive permit-granting authority.

The ZBA can either approve the proposed development as submitted, approve with conditions, or deny the project. If the town already meets the 10 percent threshold, the ZBA has the authority to

Morgan Woods, Edgartown, Massachusetts

BRUCE T. MARTIN PHOTOGRAPHY SOURCE: THE COMMUNITY BUILDERS

Morgan Woods is a 60-unit affordable property in the community of Edgartown, Massachusetts, on Martha's Vineyard. The developer, the Community Builders Inc., was able to deliver critically needed affordable rental options for the town's workforce through modular construction and a partnership that allowed for the necessary increased density as encouraged under the state's Chapter 40B law.

deny the proposal without it then heading to the Massachusetts Housing Appeals Committee.

If a municipality does not meet the 10 percent threshold and the local ZBA denies the project, or if it is approved with conditions, the developer has the option to appeal the local decision to the state's Housing Appeals Committee. This committee exists to provide an impartial review of development proposals that incorporate affordable housing, weighing both the regional need for such housing and local concerns. Unless the development poses a risk to the environment or is inconsistent with other state statutes (e.g., highway access permits, state wetlands protection requirements), the state has the authority to approve the project, thus overriding the ZBA's prior decision.

In terms of impact, it is estimated that Chapter 40B has spurred the development of more than 68,000 units across the state of Massachusetts, including 35,000 that are affordable to households with incomes below 80 percent of AMI (figure 6).

Under 40B, housing affordable to low- and moderate-income families, including multifamily rental housing, has been built in higher-income communities that had a history of excluding such development. In 1972, shortly after 40B was enacted, only four of Massachusetts's 351 cities and towns had over 10 percent of housing units affordable, a figure that has since increased tenfold to 40 communities, with many other communities nearing it.[44]

Takeaways

Massachusetts's Chapter 40B program is probably the most aggressive state policy designed to override local development approval decisions, and it is not without critics. The Pioneer Institute for Public Policy Research has summarized some of the potential ways in which Chapter 40B has not always worked as intended to promote the development of needed affordable and workforce housing:

> Some developers are using 40B as a cover to reap profits from projects that primarily cater to higher-income demographics, while some towns are doing everything they can to avoid responsibility. This has inevitably led to lengthy, drawn-out conflicts, along with heightened tensions and suspicions among local residents. In most of these disputes, the truth seems to [lie] somewhere in the middle.[45]

In addition to the criticisms about developers misusing the policy, critics have suggested that 68,000 units represent a drop in the bucket of overall development (and need) across the state over that period, and that such state overreach to achieve such a small level of output might not be justified.

It seems clear, though, that 40B has been responsible for the production of affordable housing developments that in most cases could not and would not have been built under traditional zoning approaches. This includes housing for the elderly, multifamily rental housing developments, and mixed-income condominiums and townhouses.

The impact of 40B is not limited to the affordable units it has enabled. The law has also spurred substantial market-rate housing development that would not have occurred, creating more housing choices for thousands of middle-class families and others.

A 2010 statewide referendum to repeal the law was rejected by Massachusetts residents 58 percent to 42 percent. Moreover, 40B has also inspired similar state laws in Connecticut, Rhode Island, and Illinois, although none has had nearly the impact of 40B.

Section III: Lessons Learned: How States and Local Communities Can Continue to Find Common Ground on Housing

The examples of state leadership summarized in this report illustrate a variety of ways in which states can help local communities create healthier housing markets, where supply is better matched with demand. The efforts summarized in this report do not suggest a state-led "silver bullet" nor do they imply that simply relying on one approach will lead to major progress on increasing the housing supply.

In fact, what is needed is a combination of interventions from the state, enacted with significant buy-in from a broad set of stakeholders. These should include a strong directive to assess housing needs and use zoning as a means to do so, accompanied by all the necessary incentives and flexibility to enable local jurisdictions to be successful.

Moving toward a smarter, more supportive state policy on local land use to expand housing choice and opportunity demands a delicate balancing act between the priorities of legislators representing districts that do not (currently) have a housing shortage and those whose districts do; and between meeting the broad needs of a growing number of state residents and longstanding local expectation of control over land use decision making.

There is reason for cautious optimism that a better balance can be struck, and must be to make meaningful progress to meet the nation's housing demand. Additional lessons from the case studies are as follows.

Lesson One

States can do more to empower local jurisdictions to increase housing choice and opportunity.

Whether under a Home Rule or Dillon's Rule framework, states have the ability to extend their authority into local land use and planning decisions, and they also have the ability to enable a more flexible regulatory environment for jurisdictions to enact local programs to expand housing options. When a state expressly prohibits an activity or a policy, it limits the ability of municipalities to respond to local needs and plan for sufficient housing. In Washington, for example, the state legislature expressly granted municipalities the authority to adopt property tax exemptions for affordable and workforce housing, giving municipalities a tool they did not have before. Framing the state's involvement as empowering local communities—rather than imposing requirements on them—is important for balancing local autonomy and broad goals for developing sufficient housing to meet demand.

Lesson Two

Requirements for local action should come with appropriate incentives and assistance.

When the state does impose requirements on localities, the best approaches will include assistance—both financial and technical—to help them comply with the initiative. This approach is evident in both Massachusetts and Connecticut:

financial and technical assistance is available to municipalities that commit to changes in land use and zoning that will lead to the development of more housing affordable to lower-income households. Incentives also are important for successful collaboration to happen between municipalities and the state.

Incentives include technical assistance, such as assistance with developing small area plans or revising zoning ordinances, as well as financial assistance to help offset some of the costs associated with planning and providing public services to new residents.

Lesson Three

State leadership can spur significant reductions in development costs.

From California's reduced parking requirements to Minnesota's holistic efforts to streamline the development process, an array of opportunities exist for states to eliminate burdensome and unnecessary costs associated with the production and preservation of housing, while still meeting other community goals. States can also challenge their municipalities and developers to take their own steps to bend the cost curve, as epitomized by the Minnesota Challenge to Lower the Cost of Affordable Housing.

Lesson Four

State policies should reflect local variation in housing markets and needs.

State involvement in local land use and zoning decisions can be an effective way to overcome local opposition to housing and to support the expansion of housing options. However, a statewide policy can potentially create inefficiencies or hardships for jurisdictions if it does not include flexibility to take into account local market conditions and needs. The statewide effort in Virginia to comprehensively assess local housing needs is designed to better understand the existing conditions and opportunities in dif-

ferent parts of the state and to be clear about how housing needs vary across the state. The Virginia initiative does not include a policy proposal for local land use, zoning, or development approval processes; however, it could potentially help inform the development of a flexible state policy that responds to local variation.

Lesson Five

State leadership can and must respect legitimate local- and neighborhood-level concerns.

The biggest argument against state intervention in local land use and zoning policy, and in development approval decisions, is that it preempts local authority over its own policies and planning and neglects the right of its citizens to make decisions about the type of community they want to live in. The increase in public opposition to new housing, generally, and affordable and workforce housing, specifically, reflects the intensity of concerns about the impact of new development on the character of and outlook for local neighborhoods, and an increased burden on local public schools.

Residents' concerns are often related to the changes to the physical form of the neighborhood and also the shifts in the characteristics of the population. The anxiety that some residents feel about change in their neighborhood must be recognized. Whether the issues are phrased as related to transportation, schools, open space, or pressure on existing public infrastructure or services generally, it is important that any public process to develop a statewide housing-related policy address these concerns.

Venues for voicing concerns must be accompanied by well-reasoned discussions about the importance of the state initiative and an explanation of the broad benefits of increasing housing supply and housing options. Education is key to working with localities to build support for state policy.

Section IV: Resources

The Impact of Local Land Use Policy on Housing Development

Glaeser, Edward L., and Joseph Gyourko, "The Economic Implications of Housing Supply," Zell/Lurie Working Paper #802, written for *The Journal of Economic Perspectives*, Draft of January 4, 2017.

Glaeser, Edward L., Joseph Gyourko, and Raven E. Saks, "Why Have Housing Prices Gone Up?" *American Economic Review*, Volume 95, No. 2, May 2, 2005, 329-333.

Encyclopedia of the Supreme Court of the United States, "Euclid v. Ambler Realty, 272 U.S. 365 (1926)."

Furman, Jason, "Barriers to Shared Growth: The Case of Land Use Regulation and Economic Rents." Remarks given at the Urban Institute, Washington, DC, November 20, 2015.

Ikeda, Sanford, and Emily Washington, *How Land-Use Regulation Undermines Affordable Housing*, Arlington, VA: the Mercatus Center at George Mason University, November 2015.

State Role in Local Land Use Policy

Reid, Carolina K., Carol Galante, and Ashley F. Weinstein-Carnes, "Addressing California's Housing Shortage: Lessons from Massachusetts Chapter 40B," *Journal of Affordable Housing*, Volume 25, Number 2, 2017, 241-274. National Association of Homebuilders, *Infrastructure Solutions: Best Practices from Results-Oriented States*, Washington, D.C.: NAHB, 2012.

Pendall, Rolf, "From Hurdles to Bridges: Local Land-Use Regulations and the Pursuit of Affordable Rental Housing," working paper prepared for Revisiting Rental Housing: A National Policy Summit, Joint Center for Housing Studies, Harvard University, Cambridge, MA, October 2007. www.jchs.harvard.edu/sites/jchs.harvard.edu/files/rr07-11_pendall.pdf

Karki, Tej Kumar, "Mandatory versus Incentive-Based State Zoning Reform Policies for Affordable Housing in the United States: A Comparative Assessment," *Housing Policy Debate*, 25:2, 2015, 234-262.

California Accessory Dwelling Unit Law

California Department of Housing and Community Development, "Accessory Dwelling Unit Memorandum," December 2016.

Rebecca Rabovsky, "Bill Analysis: SB 1069," California State Assembly, Committee on Housing and Community Development Committee, August 1, 2016.

California Planning and Zoning Law

Enabling legislation, California State Legislature website:
https://leginfo.legislature.ca.gov/faces/billNavClient.xhtml?bill_id=201520160AB744

Summary of AB 744 by Goldfarb Lipman Attorneys:
https://goldfarblipman.com/wp-content/uploads/2015/10/Law-Alert-State-Slashes-Parking-Requirements-for-Housing-Near-Transit-10-16-15.pdf

California Regional Housing Needs Allocation

California Department of Housing and Community Development website:
http://hcd.ca.gov/community-development/housing-element/index.shtml

California Department of Housing and Community Development, *California's Housing Future: Challenges and Opportunities, Public Draft: Statewide Housing Assessment 2025*, Sacramento, CA: State of California, January 2017, www.hcd.ca.gov/policy-research/plans-reports/docs/California's-Housing-Future-Full-Public-Draft.pdf

Connecticut Incentive Housing Zones

Connecticut Department of Housing website: www.ct.gov/doh/cwp/view.asp?a=4513&Q=530592

Klein, Evonne M., "Annual Report to the Governor and General Assembly on Incentive Housing Zones," State of Connecticut, Department of Housing, December 20, 2016, www.ct.gov/doh/lib/doh/ihz_annual_report.pdf (accessed July 24, 2017).

Partnership for Strong Communities, "The HOMEConnecticut Campaign: A Decade's Progress in Expanding Affordable Housing" pamphlet, 2016

Florida's William E. Sadowski Affordable Housing Trust Fund

Sadowski Coalition's website: www.sadowskicoalition.org/

Massachusetts Housing and Comprehensive Permitting and Zoning Appeal Law

Massachusetts Department of Housing and Economic Development website: www.mass.gov/hed/community/40b-plan/

Bluestone, Barry, Catherine Tumber, James Huessy, and Tim Davis, *The Greater Boston Housing Report Card 2016: The Trouble with Growth: How Unbalanced Economic Expansion Affects Housing*, Boston, MA: Boston Foundation, 2016

Massachusetts Smart Growth Zoning Overlay District Act

Massachusetts Department of Housing and Economic Development website: www.mass.gov/hed/community/planning/chapter-40-r.html

Bluestone, Barry, Catherine Tumber, James Huessy, and Tim Davis, *The Greater Boston Housing Report Card 2016: The Trouble with Growth: How Unbalanced Economic Expansion Affects Housing*, Boston, MA: Boston Foundation, 2016

Minnesota Challenge to Lower the Cost of Affordable Housing

Minnesota Challenge website: www.mnchallenge.com/

Minnesota Housing Finance Agency, *2015 Cost Containment Report*, September 15, 2015

Minnesota Housing Finance Agency, *2016 Cost Containment Report*, September 15, 2016

Texas Homestead Preservation District and Reinvestment Zones

Enabling legislation, Texas State Legislature website: www.statutes.legis.state.tx.us/Docs/LG/htm/LG.373A.htm

Austin Department of Neighborhood Housing and Community Development website: http://austintexas.gov/page/homestead-preservation-districts

Utah Local Redevelopment Agencies

Enabling legislation, Utah State Legislature website: https://le.utah.gov/xcode/Title17C/17C.html?v=C17C_2016051020160510

Long, Adam, "Utah Law Developments: Community Development and Renewal Agencies Act Revisions, Title 17C 20," *Utah Bar Journal* 29:4, Jul/Aug 2016, 20

Washington Multifamily Housing Tax Exemption

Enabling legislation, Washington State Legislature website: http://apps.leg.wa.gov/rcw/default.aspx?cite=84.14

Seattle Office of Housing, *City of Seattle Multifamily Property Tax Exemption Program 2016 Status Report to the City Council*, March 30, 2017

Notes

1   Winston Churchill, in a speech to the House of Commons (meeting in the House of Lords), October 28, 1943, accessed from the website of the U.K. Parliament on July 26, 2017: www.parliament.uk/about/living heritage/building/palace/architecture/palacestructure/churchill/.

2   Judge David C. Westenhaver, "Ambler Realty Co. v. Village of Euclid," 297 F. 307, 316 (N.D. Ohio 1924).

3   California Department of Housing and Community Development, California's Housing Future: Challenges and Opportunities, Public Draft: Statewide Housing Assessment 2025 (Sacramento, CA: State of California, January 2017), 34, http://www.hcd.ca.gov/policy-research/plans-reports/docs/California's-Housing-Future-Full-Public-Draft.pdf (accessed July 23, 2017).

4   Kathleen Pender, "Bay Area Building Boom May Not End Housing Shortage," San Francisco Chronicle, April 2, 2016, /www.sfchronicle.com/business/networth/article/Bay-Area-building-boom-may-not-end-housing-7223711.php.

5   Edward Glaeser, "Reforming Land Use Regulations," Brookings Institution, April 24, 2017, https://www.brookings.edu/research/reforming-land-use-regulations/.

6   Harvard University Joint Center for Housing Studies, The State of the Nation's Housing 2017 (Cambridge, MA: Harvard University, 2017).

7   Allison Charette et al., Projecting Trends in Severely Cost-Burdened Renters: 2015–2025 (Cambridge, MA; Columbia, MD: Harvard University Joint Center for Housing Studies; Enterprise Community Partners Inc., September 21, 2015), 12.

8   U.S. Census Bureau; American Community Survey, "2015 American Community Survey 1-Year Estimates," Table B25070, generated by Lisa Sturtevant using American FactFinder, http://factfinder.census.gov (26 July 2017).

9   U.S. Census Bureau and U.S. Department of Housing and Urban Development, "New Residential Construction," Table 3b, downloaded from https://www.census.gov/construction/nrc/index.html (26 July 2017). Also available at U.S. Census Bureau, Monthly New Residential Construction, June 2017 (Washington, D.C.: U.S. Census Bureau, 2017), 5.

10   Lawrence Yun, "A Troubling Shortfall of Homes," National Association of Realtors, March 2016.

11   Mac Taylor, California's High Housing Costs: Causes and Consequences (Sacramento, CA: Legislative Analyst's Office, March 17, 2015), 4.

12   U.S. Census Bureau and U.S. Department of Housing and Urban Development, "Building Permits Survey, Permits by State, Annual Data," downloaded from https://www.census.gov/construction/bps/stateannual.html (26 July 2017).

13   Joseph Gyourko and Raven Molloy, "Regulation and Housing Supply," (working paper No. 20536, National Bureau of Economic Research, Cambridge, MA, October 2014), 1.

14   David E. Bernstein, "Lochner, Parity, and the Chinese Laundry Cases," William & Mary Law Review, 41:1, Article 8, 1999, 251–252.

15   Donald L. Elliott, A Better Way to Zone: Ten Principles to Create More Livable Cities (Washington, D.C.: Island Press, 2008), 9–10.

16   John R. Nolan, "Historical Overview of the American Land Use System: A Diagnostic Approach to Evaluating Governmental Land Use Control," Pace Environmental Law Review, 23:3, Article 8, 2006, 821.

17   Jason Furman, "Barriers to Shared Growth: The Case of Land Use Regulation and Economic Rents," (remarks given at the Urban Institute, Washington, D.C., November 20, 2015), https://obamawhitehouse.archives.gov/sites/default/files/page/files/20151120_barriers_shared_growth_land_use_regulation_and_economic_rents.pdf.

18   See for example: William A. Fischel, "An Economic History of Zoning and a Cure for Its Exclusionary Effects," Urban Studies, 41:2, February 1, 2004, 317.

19   Nico Calavita and Alan Mallach, Inclusionary Housing in International Perspective: Affordable Housing, Social Inclusion, and Land Value Recapture (Cambridge, MA: Lincoln Institute of Land Policy, 2010).

20   Tej Kumar Karki, "Mandatory Versus Incentive-Based State Zoning Reform Policies for Affordable Housing in the United States: A Comparative Assessment," Housing Policy Debate, 25:2, June 25, 2014, 234.

21   Oregon has a similar statutory and regulatory framework: Goal 10 of the "Land Use Planning Act of 1973." For more information, see: https://www.oregon.gov/LCD/Pages/goals.aspx.

22   California Department of Housing and Community Development, *California's Housing Future: Challenges and Opportunities, Public Draft: Statewide Housing Assessment 2025* (Sacramento, CA: State of California, January 2017), 34, http://www.hcd.ca.gov/policy-research/plans-reports/docs/California's-Housing-Future-Full-Public-Draft.pdf (accessed July 23, 2017).

23   Mac Taylor, *Do Communities Adequately Plan for Housing?* (Sacramento, CA: Legislative Analyst's Office, March 8, 2017), 5.

24   Carolina K. Reid, Carol Galante, and Ashley F. Weinstein-Carnes, "Addressing California's Housing Shortage: Lessons from Massachusetts Chapter 40B," Journal of Affordable Housing, 25:2, 2017, 265.

25   Matthew Palm and Deb Niemeir, "The Effectiveness of Regional Housing Policy: Evidence from the San Francisco Bay Area," University of California, Davis, Center for Regional Change, April 16, 2015.

26   Partnership for Strong Communities, "The HOMEConnecticut Campaign: A Decade's Progress in Expanding Affordable Housing" pamphlet, 2016.

27   Partnership for Strong Communities. "Incentive Housing Zone (IHZ) Program." http://www.pschousing.org/homeconnecticut-program (accessed July 24, 2017).

28   David Fink, consultant to Partnership for Strong Communities, email to authors, July 18, 2017.

29   Massachusetts Department of Housing and Economic Development website: www.mass.gov/hed/community/planning/chapter-40-r.html.

30   William Reyelt, principal planner, Smart Growth Programs, Office of Sustainable Communities, Massachusetts Department of Housing and Community Development, email to authors, July 18, 2017.

31   Minnesota Housing Finance Agency, 2015 Cost Containment Report, September 15, 2015, 13.

32   Minnesota Housing Finance Agency, 2016 Cost Containment Report, September 15, 2016, 12.

33   Donna Kimura, "California Developers Win Parking Victory," Affordable Housing Finance, October 23, 2015.

34   California Department of Housing and Community Development, "Accessory Dwelling Unit Memorandum," December 2016.

35   "San Francisco Parking Supply and Utilization Study," San Francisco County Transportation Authority, 2016.

36   Rebecca Rabovsky, "Bill Analysis: SB 1069," California State Assembly, Committee on Housing and Community Development Committee, August 1, 2016.

37   The Utah law was modeled on the 1951 California Redevelopment Law, which enabled local jurisdictions to generate billions of dollars of investment in housing and other development activities. Note that in 2011 California's legislature abolished local redevelopment agencies at the behest of Governor Jerry Brown.

38   James Wood, John Downen, D.J. Benway, and Darius Li, *Regional Analysis of Impediments to Fair Housing Choice, Salt Lake County* (Salt Lake City, UT: Bureau of Economic and Business Research, David Eccles School of Business, University of Utah, May 2014), 33.

39   Jo Clifton, "City Discovers Problem with Homestead Districts," Austin Monitor, January 20, 2017.

40   Seattle Office of Housing, "City of Seattle Multifamily Property Tax Exemption Program: 2016 Status Report to the City Council," March 30, 2017, https://www.seattle.gov/Documents/Departments/Housing/HousingDevelopers/MultifamilyTaxExemption/2016_MFTE_Annual_Report_with_Attachments-Final.pdf (accessed July 21, 2017).

41   Mary Ellen Klas, "Where did $1.3 billion for affordable housing go? Florida Legislature took it," Miami Herald, March 31, 2017, http://www.miamiherald.com/news/politics-government/state-politics/article142033109.html.

42   Sadowski Housing Coalition, http://www.sadowskicoalition.org/ (accessed July 24, 2017).

43   Tej Kumar Karki, "Mandatory versus Incentive-Based State Zoning Reform Policies for Affordable Housing in the United States: A Comparative Assessment," Housing Policy Debate, 25:2, June 25, 2014, 234.

44   Carolina K. Reid, Carol Galante, and Ashley F. Weinstein-Carnes, "Addressing California's Housing Shortage: Lessons from Massachusetts Chapter 40B," Journal of Affordable Housing, 25:2, 2017, 251.

45   Will Kauppila, "Town Residents Clash with Developers over Chapter 40B Housing Law," Pioneer Institute, August 5, 2016, http://pioneerinstitute.org/blog/town-residents-clash-developers-chapter-40b-housing-law/.